AF486997

GHOST HOUSE

S.M. CORNTHWAITE'S

HollowSCREAMS
GHOST HOUSE

Hollow Screams: Day of the Dolls

ISBN: 9798469549864

Independently published

By Shannon M. Cornthwaite

Copyright © 2021

This is a work of fiction. All characters, organizations, and events portrayed in this publication are either products of the author's imagination or are used fictitiously.

No part of this publication may be reproduced, stored in a retrieval system, or transmitted, in any form or by any means without the prior written permission of the author/publisher, nor otherwise circulated in any form of binding or cover other than that in which it is published and without a similar condition being imposed on the subsequent purchaser. HOLLOW SCREAMS is a registered trademark of Shannon M. Cornthwaite.

Written by Shannon M. Cornthwaite

Cover designed by Shannon M. Cornthwaite and Catie Davis

INTRODUCTION

Somewhere in the midwestern United States, there exists a dreaded place. A place where ghosts and goblins exist. A place where monsters attack. This is a place that was built on an ancient burial site. The people who live here only dare whisper the legends which haunt the town.

In this town resides a large hollow of trees. A wooded area where the dead never find peace. This is a place that is doomed for all eternity and drives many who enter insane!

I tell you dear reader to BEWARE, because the Hollow is a real place where ghosts stalk the night and haunted houses fill the town around it. Those who dare to enter its boundaries at night and walk the paths where the hounds once ruled, shall find around them a horrid sight as the dead are brought back to life.

Enter if you dare, because at night, the Hollow SCREAMS!

Dedicated to my children: Ally, Duke, and Marissa

Special thanks to Jennifer Merrick

Thirteen-year-old, Jake Whitney just moved into a new house, far away from all his friends. His dad just got a new job as principal at the school Jake will soon be attending. As an only child, Jake didn't really have anyone close to his age that he could talk to about this, that would understand. They just moved into an old house in a neighborhood on the edge of town. There were a few other kids in the area, that he'd seen when he got to town, but he hasn't met any of them yet.

The house he and his family moved into, was built sometime in the 1800's. He had overheard the realtor tell his parents as his dad just nodded in agreement. It was big with an upstairs, an attic, a main floor, and a basement. There were 5 bedrooms in the house and 2 bathrooms. It had a huge living room, a large dining room, a kitchen that was big enough to fit a breakfast table in, and lots of windows.

Being that the house had 5 bedrooms, the family decided that Mr. and Mrs. Whitney would take the largest as their bedroom, while Jake would get the second largest as his. The third largest would be turned into a guest room while one of the smaller rooms would be made into Mr. Whitney's home office. That just left the smallest of the rooms to decide what to do with. Eventually, Mrs. Whitney decided to turn it into her hobby room, where she could do her sewing and craft making.

The main bathroom was on the first floor with the living room, dining room, and kitchen. It had an old cast iron tub with legs that looked like lion feet and a pipe that ran up from the faucet to the shower head. Most newer houses had the pipes for the plumbing hidden within the wall by the shower, but older houses left it all exposed. There was a metal ring around the top of the shower for a curtain to be pulled around, which was attached to the same pipe that led up to the shower head.

The house had hardwood floors that had to be cleaned regularly, otherwise dust would cover them, constantly. Being that the house was so old, the floorboards creaked and squeaked with every step. No matter how quiet you were trying to be while walking, the boards would always alert anyone within the house of movement. The Whitney's tried to use large area rugs where they could and long narrow rugs for hallways and other walkway areas, but that still didn't help with the dust problem or the creaky boards.

The stairs leading to the second floor, creaked even more than the floorboards did. With every step, you could hear a squeak, creak, or thump. Even if you didn't live in this house, and were only visiting, you learned almost immediately that there was no way you could possibly sneak up on anyone there.

The basement which you could get to by way of a door in the kitchen that opened to a staircase, was creepy no matter what age you were. It was dark, dusty, and filled with cobwebs. Just looking down there sent chills up Jake's spine. His mom didn't really like it either, but that's where the hook ups were for the washer and dryer, so she'd have to get used to it if the family was going to have clean clothes.

Jake's room was upstairs and to the right at the end of the hallway, while his parents' room was at the other end of the hallway, to the left of the staircase. The other three rooms were laid out between the two with a bathroom right next to the right-hand side of the staircase. Next to it, was a large closet where his mom decided to keep the bathroom towels, wash rags, extra soap, toilet paper and vacuum cleaner for the upstairs' rugs. It was large enough, that an adult could fit inside, between the shelves and the door.

The doors for all the rooms were heavy and creaked when you opened them. Their hinges were old as well and seemed as if they hadn't been oiled in years, because they too squeaked when the doors moved. The doorknobs were made of brass and looked like they were originals, installed around the time the house was built.

Shortly after moving in, Mr. Whitney went through the entire house with a can of oil and used it on all the door hinges and knobs to try and cut back on the squeaking. But it made little difference. It was just something they were going to have to live with.

Jake's bedroom, since it was a double corner room which took up one side of the upstairs, had windows which nearly filled three of the four walls. In it, he had his bunk beds, which he had for when his friends would stay the night. He also had a chest of drawers as his mom called it, but he just referred to it as a dresser with his tv sitting atop it right next to the door to his room. Next to the head end of his bunk beds, he had a bookcase where he kept a stack of comic books, old baseball cards, and some model cars his dad and he built when he was younger.

One of Jake's favorite past times was scaring people and pulling pranks, so he had several Halloween masks laying about his room. Some were creepy clown masks, others were monsters, he had a hockey mask and several others. He also kept containers of home-made slime and fake hands as well as rubber snakes, mice and spiders on another bookcase which stood against the wall at the foot end of his bunk beds. His closet was right across the room from his bunk, along the inside wall. It was a long walk-in closet and deep as well. He kept his shoes, shirts, baseball equipment as well as some other stuff in there.

Even though his room had windows on three of the four walls, he still had places where he was able to hang posters. Like most boys his age, Jake had posters which featured his favorite superheroes as well as his favorite baseball team, which was the Chicago Cubs. There were also posters which represented his favorite movies, like Ghostbusters and Back to the Future.

One of the first pieces of decoration he put up when he got moved into his new room, was an assortment of glow-in-the-dark ceiling stars and planets. He had gotten a few packs at the store in his hometown a few years ago and had them all over his ceiling at the old house. He loved it, so he did the same thing here, but since his new room was so much bigger than his old room, his parents had to get him several more packs.

He and his family had been living in the house now, for about a week or so, and they spent most of that time unpacking, so Jake hadn't had a chance to go out and meet any of the kids his own age yet. But that was about to change. Now that he had all his stuff unpacked and put away, he was ready to go outside and throw his ball around. Maybe, just maybe, he'd catch the attention of a kid his age and they'd strike up a friendship, or at the very least, a conversation.

"Mom! I'm gonna go out and throw the ball around in the front yard," he called out as he ran down the stairs with his ball and mitt in hand.

"Ok Hun, just let me know before you leave the yard ok."

"Will do," he called back as he swung open the front door and darting outside, slamming it shut behind him.

Jake was in his front yard, throwing his baseball up into the air and catching it in his mitt, for just a few minutes when a kid came out of the house across the street. He looked as if he were about Jake's age, and he held a mitt in his hand and walked over to Jake.

The kid had curly reddish-brown hair under a Cardinals ball cap with chubby cheeks. He was kinda short and a little chunky but not overweight. He had cut off blue jean shorts and a Minecraft t-shirt with the sleeves cut off. The shoes he wore were low top sneakers with socks that rose midway up his calf.

"Hey," the boy said. "Mind if I play catch with ya?"

"Sure. But you gotta leave that hat at home," he joked with a smile. "What's your name," Jake asked curiously while tossing his ball in the other boy's direction.

Catching it in his mitt with his left hand and chuckling at the mention of his hat, the boy chomped on a wad of bubble gum and replied, "Eric, and don't tell me you're a Cubby fan. What's yours?"

"My name's Jake and I sure am so Card merch aint welcome around here," he joked once more. "How old are you?"

Taking the ball out of his mitt and tossing it to Jake, he piped up, "I'm twelve, I'll be thirteen in a few months! How about you?"

Jake caught the ball in his mitt off to the side and threw it back immediately. "Just turned thirteen a few months ago. Have you lived here long?"

"All my life. The neighborhood's ok, I guess. But I don't really care much for the school."

"Why? What's wrong with the school?"

They continued tossing the ball back and forth while getting to know each other and Jake learning about his new home. "Well, the kids are pretty cool for the most part, and the teachers are ok I guess, but the principal is really strange. Well, our old principal anyway. He left town as soon as school let out for the Summer. He lived here, before you guys moved in."

"Weird, I didn't know that. The lady who sold my parents the house didn't say anything about that," Jake uttered. "My dad just got hired on as the new principal. Why'd the old one leave?"

"I don't know," Eric shrugged. "He started at the beginning of the school year last year and he was ok, starting out. But as the year went on, you could tell he was just starting to lose it, ya know. He started showing up late to school and just got more and more on edge."

Eric continued on as the boys through the ball back and forth, "The times I saw him at the end of the year, he looked like he hadn't shaved in a long time or combed his hair and his eyes looked like he hadn't slept in weeks. There were times he would yell at kids in the hall for just talking to their friends. Teachers started getting on edge any time he was around too. The first morning of summer break, I came outside and there was a For Sale sign in the yard. I guess he left in the middle of the night or something."

"Weird," Jake responded.

"Yeah, before he moved in though, the house had been empty, for a long time. Rumor has it, the place is haunted."

"You're messing with me right," Jake said while rolling his eyes. "There's no such thing as ghosts. Besides, we've been here a week and I haven't seen anything."

Eric shrugged as he grabbed the ball he just caught from his mitt, "Well, that's what I heard. But who knows, I've never been in there, so I don't know."

"Well, you wanna come in?"

Eric hesitated and looked at the house suspiciously. He took his hat in his hand and wiped the sweat from his brow, "Uhhh sure, ok."

The two boys ran up to the house with Jake charging through the front door with Eric right behind him. Jake's mom was sitting in the living room, reading a book when they burst in and peeked over the top of it toward the boys, "Shut the door please."

Shutting it behind them, Jake looked over at his mom and introduced her to Eric. Right after the two said their hellos to each other, Mr. Whitney skipped down the stairs. "Well Jake, that didn't take ya very long. I see you've made a new friend."

"Yeah Dad, this is Eric, he lives across the street. He said the old principal of the school lived here before we moved in."

"Oh, hmmm. The realtor neglected to mention that when we looked at the house. Interesting. So, Eric, do you have a last name, or do you just have the one, like Madonna or Cher?"

The boy chuckled at Mr. Whitney's joke. "Eric Sanders sir."

"Eric Sanders Sir? Interesting name," Jake's dad joked in response.

"No, no. Just Eric Sanders."

"Ah! That makes a little more sense. Pleased to meet you Eric Sanders, I'm your new principal Mr.

Whitney. What a coincidence, I was just looking over the student files, learning about my new students, and yours' was the last one I read. Very interesting stuff Mr. Sanders. I hope you won't give me as hard a time as you have your teachers. And we're going to have to do something about that hat. There'll be no mention of that team in my school."

Eric stood there in shock, not sure what to say, until Jake piped up, "He's messing with you dude. He does this all the time. He just wanted to see how you'd react."

A sly smile crossed Mr. Whitney's face as Eric let out a gasp of relief. He wasn't sure what was in his file, but he didn't think he had given any of his teachers a hard time. Eric was a good kid, all though he tends to get quite excited at times... well most of the time.

"I was just going to show Eric around," Jake told his dad.

"Ok, well you two have a good time," Mr. Whitney said with a smile. "And I'll see you at school next week right," he said while looking over his glasses at Eric sternly before again presenting a smile across his face and swiping his hand over the boy's head to ruffle the hair under his cap with his palm, then walked to the kitchen.

The two boys went upstairs and straight to Jake's bedroom. The floorboards and stairs creaked and squeaked under their feet. Eric was amazed by how normal the inside of the house, that had such a bad reputation looked.

The Whitney's sure made it look cozy and welcoming. It was strange, when he first walked up the steps to the door, the hairs on his neck stood at attention and goosebumps covered his arms. But once he got inside and met Jake's parents then saw how welcoming the inside was, he was put at ease.

In Jake's room, Eric looked around at all his new friend's stuff. He was a little spooked by the clown masks because that was one thing Eric hated, was clowns. But everything else seemed cool.

The boys shared a lot of common interests. They both liked baseball and comic books. But, where Jake liked the Cubs, Eric was more of a Cardinals fan. While Jake liked DC comics, Eric was more into Marvel.

"So, where'd you guys move here from," Eric asked while skimming through Jake's comic book collection.

For a moment there was silence, then Eric turned to his new friend. **"RAHHH!"**

"Ahhh!" he jumped back in surprise. There was a horrific evil looking clown two inches from his face!

Pulling off the mask, Jake laughed at the reaction he got from his new friend. "Oh man, you should 'a seen the look on your face! I wish I had a camera," he laughed.

"Not funny dude! I hate clowns!"

"I know, I could tell by the way you looked at my masks. We moved here from Sandlewood," Jake said as he fixed his hair with his hand and hung the mask back up. "Have you ever heard of it? It's about three hours north of here by car."

"No. Is it a big city? Or is it small like this place?"

"Kinda in between really. It was small enough that my friends and I could ride our bikes everywhere, but big enough that everyone didn't know all your business."

"Yeah, word does tend to spread like wildfire anytime you pick your nose around here," Eric said returning his attention to Jake's comics.

"So, this place is that small huh," Jake asked. "I wasn't sure how big the town was, since we came straight here, and I haven't been able to ride my bike around."

"Why don't I go get my bike and I can show you around," Eric exclaimed as he slid Jakes comics back onto their shelf.

"Sure! That sounds great! I've been stuck at home since we moved in, and man does it get boring."

Eric jumped to his feet and got ready to dart out the doorway, but just as he took a single step forward, Jake's bedroom door slammed shut.

Both boys flinched at the sound and seemed quite confused by what had happened. They looked at each other and then back at the door. Chills shot up their backs and they weren't quite sure what to make of it.

"Was that you," Eric asked, looking dead eye at Jake.

"Uh uh," he shook his head in response.

Their eyes got big as they inched toward the door. Jake hesitantly reached out his hand to turn the knob when suddenly they heard a loud knocking come from it that sent them jumping backward.

"Guys," Jakes dad called to them from the other side. "What's goin on in there?"

Jake grabbed the knob and turned it, but the door wouldn't budge. "Uh I don't know dad, the door just slammed shut and now I can't get it open."

Through the doorknob, he could feel his dad jiggle it on the other side before he released and took a step back. He could tell his dad was trying to get the door open but was having absolutely no luck.

"Ok guys," his dad called through the door. "Stand back, I'm gonna try to force it open!"

The boys moved to the other side of the room just before Jake yelled out, "Ok dad!"

They could see the knob turn and then the door shook with a thump. A few seconds passed before the door shook again with another thump. A few more seconds passed when suddenly they heard a thump and the door swung open.

"I guess I must have put to much oil on the hinges. A breeze coming through your window must have been just enough to catch the door just right," Mr. Whitney said rubbing his shoulder due to the force it took to get the door open and motioning toward the opened windows around Jake's room. "I'll get my tools and fix the hinges, so this doesn't happen again, ok. We'll have to get a door stop or something so the wind doesn't keep blowing your door shut every time you have the windows open."

"Sounds good," Jake replied. "Would it be ok if Eric showed me around town today?"

"Yeah," his dad responded. "Just be home in time for dinner."

With that, both boys darted out the doorway and down the stairs. "Slow it down guys," Mr. Whitney called out. "You don't wanna trip and fall down the stairs."

Without responding, both boys slowed it down and hopped down the stairs. Once to the bottom, Jake's mom stepped through the entry way to the living room. "Everything alright up there," she asked.

"Ya," Jake answered. "Dad thinks he just added to much oil to the hinges and the door got stuck."

"Don't worry," Mr. Whitney called down. "I'm fixin it!"

"Dad, said it was ok for me to go around town with Eric as long as I'm back by dinner," Jake stated with his hand aiming his thumb over his shoulder, pointing behind him and up the stairs to his dad.

"Ok," she said before they ran out the door, leaving it standing wide open. "Don't forget to shut the door," she muttered to herself.

Jake and Eric spent the day riding around town on their bikes. Eric gave his new friend the grand tour, as some would say. They checked out the theater. Eric told him that legend has it the place was haunted by a ghost who'd scare anyone who came in there at night.

The minimart, a couple of the towns few restaurants, and the park were all on their tour route. It was nothing special, but all the legends and ghost stories people told about the place made up for it. On their journey, they came across three of Eric's friends at the park.

"Hey guys, what'cha doin," Eric questioned casually as he and Jake pulled up.

"Just skippin rocks in the fountain," a blonde-haired boy answered without even turning around.

The boy had on a white t-shirt with red and black stripes. His shorts where the kind people wore to the gym or when playing basketball. His shoes were high-top sneakers with ankle high socks.

There was another boy with spikey brown hair standing next to him. He had on a green tank top and jeans that you could tell someone had cut to make them into shorts. On his feet were a dirty old pair of at one time, white high-top sneakers. These were the kind made of fabric with where the heal and the toe were made from a completely different material and a circle with a star inside decorated the side by his ankle.

Next to him, a girl stood with shoulder length red hair and freckles splashed across her cheeks and nose. She had on short tan shorts which stopped about mid-thigh and a yellow tank top with what appeared to be a bathing suit underneath. On her feet, she wore a pair of sandals that were held on securely by a strap.

The three each had rocks in their hands and were slinging them across the large fountain in the middle of the park, trying to get them to skip. They would take turns skimming them across the water by slinging their arms from their sides. Most of the time their rocks would do exactly what they wanted them to, but occasionally they'd come across one or two that would just got straight to the bottom.

The only one to look back at them was the girl. She glanced over at Jake and smiled. "Who's your friend Eric," she asked.

"Guys, I'd like you to meet Jake," Eric said without waiting for his friends to turn around. "He just moved here, and his dad is going to be our new principal. They moved into Mr. Gradey's house."

With that revelation, the trio stopped what they were doing and turned to face the boys. The kid with the blonde hair and the kid with the spikey hair, both had their mouths gaped open in astonishment.

"You moved into Shady Gradey's house," the girl piped up in surprise.

"Shady Gradey," Jake confusingly questioned.

"Yeah," Eric chimed in. "That's what everyone calls him. There's ummm... some things I didn't tell you about, that happened when he lived there."

"I heard he locked up kids who got sent to the office, in his basement," the spikey haired kid excitedly announced.

"My older brother said he saw him in there arguing with himself one night, like he was going crazy or something," the girl added.

"Guys," Eric announced to get their attention. "I woke up in the middle of the night one time and saw him running around the outside of his house in his underwear. He was pacing back and forth, pulling at his hair, and shaking. He was completely out of his mind!"

"That's why we call him Shady Gradey, cuz he always seemed like he was up to some shady stuff," the blonde kid added.

"Jake," Eric announced, raising his hand in the direction of each of his friends. "These are Blake with the spikey hair, Hudson's the blonde, and Stephanie I'm sure you can guess which one she is."

"Hey guys, nice to meet you," Jake responded.

"I'm showing Jake around town," Eric established. "You guys wanna get on your bikes and join us?"

"Sure," Stephanie exclaimed as she walked over to her yellow beach cruiser.

The other two boys skipped one last rock a piece and turned to grab their bikes. Together, all five kids road off on their two wheelers, with Blake and Hudson taking the lead as Jake, Eric and Stephanie road side by side.

"Has Eric told you about our local legends," Stephanie asked as she turned her head to face Jake.

"A little bit," Jake chuckled. "He told me; my house is haunted. Or at least that's what people say anyway. But I haven't seen anything. And he told me about the theater."

"Did he tell you, the entire town is built on an ancient Indian burial ground," Stephanie asked spookily.

"No, seriously?"

"Yeah," Eric chimed in. "At least, that's what everyone says."

"Have you seen the cemetery," Stephanie asked.

Confused, Jake shook his head. "No. What's so special about the cemetery?"

"That's the heart of the town. That's where it all started. There's a wooded area around it, that people call the Hollow. A lot of really bad things happened out there shortly after the town was founded. People have seen ghosts in the cemetery at night and heard howling in the hollow. But there aren't any wolves around here and dogs stay as far away from there as they can."

"Let's take him to the clearing," Blake suggested.

"The clearing," Jake questioned.

"Yeah, it's a place in the Hollow where we hang out," Eric told him. "No one else ever goes out there 'cept for us and the occasional four-wheeler clearing the paths. It's pretty close to the creek and it's really not that far from where we live."

The five kids rode their bikes through the woods, on dirt trails. The spot they were heading too, was pretty far from the park they started at. The edge of the woods bordered the neighborhood that all five kids lived in. And the cemetery was nearby.

They had to ride their bikes about a mile into the woods, which took them almost five minutes from the time they entered the tree line. When they finally reached the spot, it was a secluded area within the woods, that had been cleared of trees and plants almost as if nothing would grow there. There was a canopy of branches from other trees, which drooped over the clearing like a natural umbrella.

Very little light pierced the branches overhead, which left it quite dark underneath with only spots where the sun's rays reached to the ground. Within the clearing, there were tires hanging by ropes from branches, poorly constructed benches that you could tell kids had built, and old large wooden spool they had standing up like a table in the center.

"Whoa! Did you guys do all this," Jake asked with astonishment.

"Some of it," Stephanie responded. "But most of it was done before we started coming here."

"This has been a place of sanctuary for kids around here for years," Blake announced as he climbed a wooden ladder that was nailed into a tree to reach a platform which was made of wood and sat atop several of the branches about 15 feet off the ground.

"It's been here since my mom was a kid," Eric said as he swung on one of the tire swings. "She and her friends use to come back here. It kinda gets passed down from generation to generation."

"When one group of kids just grow up and stop coming here," Stephanie added as she dropped the kickstand of her bike and relaxed on the seat. "They show a new group of kids how to get here."

Hudson piped up as he followed Blake up the ladder, "It started years ago when a group of kids were constantly being bullied. Every day, a group of bullies would find them no matter where they were in town and just start causing trouble."

"So, the kids who were being bullied," Blake chimed in from the platform above the trio, "started coming out to the woods. They found this spot where nothing would grow, and they turned it into their sanctuary."

"This was their safe space. No one else knew about it, "Stephanie continued. "Most other kids in town, don't go this far into the woods. If they do, they go straight to the creek on the other end of the woods. But its only safe during the day."

"This place is pretty cool," Jake said while admiring everything inside the clearing. "So do you guys have a problem with bullies and why is it only safe during the day?"

"No, not really. There's a couple of creeps in town who tease everyone," Eric stated as he started climbing the ladder to the platform, answering Jake's first question. "But they don't actually hurt anyone. "They're more annoying than anything."

"I see," said Jake as he rolled his eyes. "I guess every town has some. And what about the other part?"

"This is part of the Hollow," Blake called down. "No one ever comes into these woods at night."

After a few minutes, Jake walked over to the ladder and got ready to climb to the platform. However, before he started up, he looked over at Stephanie. She was just sitting there on her bike, keeping a close eye on the boys above her but not joining in.

"You comin," Jake ask as he pointed upward.

Uh uh," Stephanie replied shaking her head. "Not a big fan of heights."

Jake then climbed the ladder and at the top of it stepped onto the platform. It was a wooden base with crates for sitting on and a railing made of boards and branches to keep them from falling over the side. There was a rope up there with knots tied into it that hung from an even higher branch, they would drop down to the ground so they could just swing down it rather than climb back down the ladder.

The four old friends spent the rest of the day in the clearing getting to know Jake, while Jake was also getting to know them as well. He told them about his family and the town he came from.

The four filled him in on the town and all the weird things that happen there. Things like the Grassman of the Hollow, the Hounds, all the haunted houses and buildings as well as what happened in the Hollow way back when the town was first forming, among other things. The town of Decatur has so many legends and so much weird stuff that happens regularly.

As the sun began to drop to meet the trees, The kids decided it was time to get home. Being that they all lived in the same neighborhood, they rode their bikes together in the same direction. When the group would come up on one of their houses, the kid who lived in that house would break off from the rest, park their bike in their garage or chain it to the porch and head inside for dinner to be ready and waiting on them.

The first to break off was Blake. He lived right on the edge of the block. It was the first house you came to as you left the woods. After that was Hudson who lived about halfway down the street. Stephanie and Eric lived right next to each other, with Jake of course residing across the street from them.

"I'll see you guys tomorrow ok," Jake called out to his new friends as he pulled his bike into the yard and locked it up on his front porch.

"Of course," Eric shouted back.

Stephanie turned, having just put her bike away and called out to Jake, "See you tomorrow!"

As Jake opened the door and stepped inside his house, he was hit in the face with the smell of homemade chicken pot pie, his favorite. "I'm home," he called out."

"Oh good," his mom replied. "I hope you're hungry, I made your favorite!"

"Starving," Jake exclaimed.

"Did you have fun with your new friend," his dad asked as he came down the stairs from his office.

"Yeah! Eric introduced me to a few other kids too and we hung out in the woods. They told me about all this freaky stuff that happens in Decatur, and about the principal who use to live in our house."

"So, are we going to meet these other new friends before school starts up next week," his dad asked while sitting down in his usual spot, at the head of the dinner table.

"I don't know, probably. They might come over tomorrow," Jake shrugged as his mom stopped him from sitting down and directed him to the kitchen sink to wash his hands.

That night as Jake lay in bed trying to sleep, the house had fallen quiet. It was late, and his parents had gone to bed long before him. It was so quiet in fact, not a single sound could be heard through his open bedroom windows. Not a lone creature stirred outside.

It was too quiet for Jake. He was used to the sounds of traffic, dogs barking, and stray cats; sounds of a larger city. But Decatur was extremely quiet at night. Quiet as death, he thought. That is, until the creak of floorboards downstairs broke the silence.

Creeeaaak

One creak downstairs could just be because the house is old. It wasn't necessarily out of the usual for old houses to creak in the night for no apparent reason, Jake knew this. The house he lived in before his family moved here, was old and it creaked.

Creeeeaaak

Another creak, but that wasn't out of the usual either. However, the creaks seemed to be moving. Jake could understand if the same spot was creaking as things shifted in the night from the cooling of the ground and what not, but moving creaks? He wasn't so sure about that.

CREAK... SQUEAK... CREAK... SQUEAK

His eyes shot open. Now it wasn't sounding like normal old house creaks. Now it was sounding more like someone walking across the floor downstairs. Jake sat up in his bed and listened to the sounds from downstairs closely. He could almost track the position of whoever or whatever it was, and where they were going.

The creaking started in the kitchen. Then it moved into the dining room. Now it was in the living room. What was going on? He thought to himself. He didn't hear either of his parents go downstairs. He hadn't seen them either. It was a straight shot line of sight from his bed, out his bedroom door, to the staircase and his parents' bedroom down the hall.

He looked, and their door was still shut. Surely, if one of his parents had gotten up in the night, they would have left their door open, so they didn't have to mess with it on their way back. He continued to listen as the creaks and squeaks traveled all the way to the foot of the stairs and stopped briefly.

Jake's heart started thumping in his chest, faster and faster. He could feel it pounding inside him. **THUMP THUMP THUMP THUMP!** There was someone else in his house and they were right at the foot of the stairs. What should he do?

7

Should he get up and try to see who or what it was? No, the floorboards would creak and squeak under him as he moved and alert the trespasser. Maybe he should call out for his parents. No, they were sound asleep. By the time one of them got up and came to check on him, the intruder would either be long gone or right in front of him.

It started moving again, the creaks and squeaks were now coming closer. He could hear them move but this time, they weren't going across the downstairs floor. Now they were coming up the stairs.

Jake was frozen stiff and unsure what to do. His eyes grew wider and wider with each creek and squeak. Sweat beaded across his forehead and slid down his face. Higher and higher they climbed, but he couldn't make out their appearance just yet. It was far too dark, and they were still too low on the stairs.

CREAK! SQUEAK! CREAK! SQUEAK!

He quickly fell back into his bed and pulled his blanket up to his chin. There was nothing else he could do. He wasn't prepared to fight off an intruder by himself. His eyes remained locked on the top of the staircase down the hall.

CREAK! SQUEAK! CREAK! SQUEAK!

He could make out a dark figure step up to the second floor, at the top of the stairs. It appeared to be a woman, but he couldn't make out any details, it was far too dark. Jake noticed that she was beginning to turn in his direction, so he quickly clinched his eyes shut and laid as stiff as a board.

CREAK! SQUEAK! CREAK! SQUEAK!

He could hear her moving his way. She was getting closer and closer to his room. Jake could hear every step she took as the floorboards creaked and squeaked under her. Just before the noises stopped just outside his doorway, he cracked open his eyes. It wasn't much, just enough so that he could see through his eye lashes. But to whoever was there, he would appear asleep.

He saw the figure step into his room. He still couldn't make out her features though, but he could tell it was a woman. She had straight long hair and wore a dress. This obviously couldn't be his mother, because she had short hair and hated dresses, rarely ever wearing them. He closed his eyes briefly as they were beginning to get heavy. But when he opened them up again, she was standing directly next to the head of his bed, inches from his face!

The sun streamed through Jake's bedroom windows. It was the next morning and Jake's eye lids flickered before opening. The sunlight hit his eyes and he rubbed the sleep from them, before sitting up in bed. As he turned and dropped his feet on the floor, he hesitated, remembering what he'd seen and heard the night before. Had the strange woman been a dream?

He wasn't sure what to think. The sounds and the look of the woman from the night before, felt so real. If it was a dream, he thought it was likely due to the stories his new friends told him earlier that day. That was probably it, his mind was just playing tricks on him, because of those stories.

He sat on the edge of his bed and performed a stretch and a yawn. He lifted his toes off the floor and wiggled them in his socks. This was his morning ritual as soon as he woke up every day.

For whatever reason, his toes always felt slightly stiff in the mornings, and he needed to wiggle them to wake them up, for lack of a better term. He wore socks to bed because he could never keep his feet under the blanket and his toes would always get cold no matter how hot it was.

He turned his head and looked out the window at the sun shining brightly in the sky. He felt something brush against his foot and quickly looked down. It was a marble and it had rolled from somewhere; he really wasn't sure where it came from, but it rolled to his foot. He was about to reach down and pick it up, but a small hand reached out from under his bed and grabbed it!

"Whoa," he muttered as shot back and quickly brought his feet back atop the bed. "What the heck was that?!"

Jake was a little scared now. He was already slightly on edge after seeing the lady in his room the night before or dream or whatever it was. But now, there was someone under his bed. Nervously, he waited a moment to gather himself. "There's someone under my bed," he thought.

A creaking noise came from below him. His throat gulped as he wasn't sure what to do. He held his knees pressed tightly into his chest as nerves took hold.

"Who's there," he asked softly but firmly.

His bat stood at the foot of his bed, leaning against it. As soon as he spotted it from the corner of his eye, he abruptly reached across his bed and grabbed it. He took hold of the wooden bat in both hands and brought the fat end up to his cheek. Gripping it tightly, he was ready to swing at anything that came out from under there.

"You better come out right now or I'm gonna crack your skull," he ordered while keeping his eyes to the side of his bed.

A moment passed. Then two. He was getting tired of waiting for whoever it was to come out. He looked over the edge of the bed again, this time with the top of his bed pointed down toward the floor. He held over him with both hands ready to club the first thing that popped out from under there.

He took a deep breath and slid onto his stomach, moving the bat to his side. Placing one hand on the edge of the bed, and holding his bat with the other, he slowly poked his head down to look under the bed and find out who was under there. Gradually, his head inched down, lower and lower until his hair fell to the floor and his eyebrows hovered at the edge of his bedframe.

Jake took another deep breath and shot his head downward. His eyes nearly bulged from their sockets when he saw what awaited him. His heart was racing, and fear shot along his spine. Heavy breathing forced his body to raise and lower quickly against his mattress. For a moment, time stood still.

What he found under his bed, was so disturbing that he couldn't find the words to describe it. His heart thumped rapidly against his chest as he lost all ability to remember how to breath. His body went stiff, and he lost all sense of composure.

It was empty under there, save for a few dust bunnies and the very marble which had rolled into his foot. There was no one under his bed. His eyes must have been playing tricks on him. Being that he had just woken up, he wasn't a bit surprised by this as he finally let out a breath of relief and grabbed the marble before rising back up.

As he sat there, he began to get the feeling he was being watched. A cold chill slithered its way up his back. He could feel cold dead eyes watching him from behind.

The temperature in the room seemed to drop in an instant as he froze.

His pupils inched to the corner of his eyes, hoping to catch a glimpse at whatever sat behind him. He felt a lump in his throat as he held his breath and swallowed. He once again tightly grabbed hold of his bat and spun around, bring it over his heady ready to strike.

He was surprised when he saw what had been behind him staring at him. The moment his eyes met it, he knew he was just being jumpy for no reason. You see, the thing which sat behind him, staring at him was nothing to be concerned with, it was just a bird that was propped along the ledge of the windowsill next to his bed.

He smiled at it and took a deep breath. He was being far too jumpy, especially first thing in the morning, he thought to himself. He sat his bat back down on his bed and returned his attention to the marble.

After looking at it for a moment or two and tossing it into the air before catching it in the same hand, Jake got out of bed and got dressed for the day. About the time that he pulled his shirt over his head, the doorbell rang. His mom answered the door, to find Eric and Stephanie standing on the other side.

"Jake," his mom called up to him. "Your friends are here to see you!"

He stepped out of his room to the top of the stairs and looked down at the doorway. "Hey guys, come on up!"

With that, Mrs. Whitney opened the door wider and welcomed the two kids inside her house. Eric led the way to the stairs, as Stephanie hesitated before stepping foot into the house. After a second or two of leaning over the entryway to peek inside, she finally stepped in and followed Eric.

As they made their way up the staircase, Stephanie couldn't help but look around. Her head swiveled from side to side anxiously. She wasn't sure what she expected from the inside of the house, but she wanted to be ready in case something were to jump out at her.

"Hey guys," Jake greeted as the pair reached the top of the stairs. "What's up," he asked as he led his friends to his room.

"Nothin much," Eric piped up. "Just wanted to come over and see what you were up to. Plus, Steph's never been inside here before, so she was curious."

Stephanie took a cautious look around Jake's room as they entered. She had heard all the different stories about the house, so she was on edge. Her body was tense with the idea that something was going to jump out at her. It took a few minutes for her to relax and just hang out with Eric and Jake.

Eventually, Jake's bookcase full of model cars, comic books and baseball stuff caught her eye. Stephanie's shoulders finally fell and she no longer felt tense. Instead, she was now curious wanted to take a closer look at all of Jake's stuff.

"What'cha got goin on today," Stephanie asked as she crept over to his bookcase and examined everything. Though she was a bit more relaxed, her head remained on a swivel waiting for something to jump out at them.

"Not much," Jake shrugged. "Mainly just hangin out. What'd you guys have in mind?"

"We didn't really have anything in mind either," Eric expressed.

"You guys wanna play some video games," Jake asked while walking to his shelf that was filled with all the necessary entertainment.

"Sounds good to me," Stephanie perked up, returning her attention to Jake.

Jake had a big enough tv and enough controllers, that all three of them were able to play together. They decided on an online shooter game, where they plaid against other users from all over the world in a virtual battle. It was one of the most popular games out at that time and the three friends decided to have each other's back, working together as a team.

About an hour into the game, the three were extremely into it. Their adrenaline was pumping, and their fingers flew between the buttons on their control pads. Their voices carried down the hall as they frantically tried to communicate with each other to keep the opposing players away.

As they got carried away with the gameplay, Eric felt the hairs on the back of his neck stand straight. It felt like someone was breathing down on him from behind. He took his hand from the controller for a split second to swat whatever it was away and returned it to hammer his buttons.

Stephanie was the next to feel something as her thumbs frantically darted back and forth across her controller, she felt the hair at the back of her head sweep to the side. It was almost as if someone had taken their hand and brushed it out of the way. "Did one of you just touch my hair," she asked without taking her eyes off the screen.

"No," Jake chuckled, not even looking at her. "How could we? We've been playing just as hard as you."

"I felt something too," Eric chimed in.

About that time, the internet lost connection and the trio all let out a sigh of disappointment at the same time. Right before Jake got up to reset the internet router, the tv mysteriously shut itself off. On the screen, the kids could only see their own four reflections staring back at them. Wait... four reflections? There were only three of them in the room.

They each went stiff as their hearts began to pound faster and faster in their chests. Not a single breath was taken between them. Their eyes locked onto the fourth image reflected at them. It was the reflection of a boy, pale in complexion and he sat there, staring at the screen.

Their skin went cold as goosebumps trailed up their arms. Not even one of them was willing to move. Their eyes went wide with fright. They were way too scared. Eventually they each turned their heads to look behind them at the fourth figure, at the same time.

The trio slowly turned their heads. Shivers crawled up their spines. Chills shot through them. Who was that in the reflection? None of them had ever seen the kid before. As their heads turned to look, their eyes met a disturbing sight.

There was no one there! Were their minds playing a trick on them? What had they seen in the reflection of the tv? Who was that and where'd he go? It couldn't have just been their imagination because they had all seen it.

"Whoa," Eric gasped. "Did you guys see the same thing I did?"

"Uh huh," Stephanie slowly nodded in agreement with her eyes still wide.

"Who... who was that" Jake asked with a stutter.

The friends surprisingly stared at each other for a few moments. It was so quiet; you could hear a pin drop. The sun continued to shine through the windows. No one moved for what seemed like forever. The door to Jake's room squeaked against its henges as it swayed slightly back and forth in the breeze that came through his window.

Though the temperature outside was in the mid 70's, a nice Summer Day; the temperature inside seemed to drop. Their faces felt cold as fear channeled their blood to other parts of their bodies. The air in the room went still. The door stopped swaying and creaking. Not a sound could be heard and not a breath was taken for the longest time.

BOOM!

The television and game system came on in an explosion of loud gun fire and bombs going off. All three kids nearly jumped out of their skin simultaneously. And each of them let out a YELP or some other sound of excited heart racing reaction.

Though they each briefly panicked from the massive jump scare that nearly launched them into the air, they recovered quickly. Jake grabbed his controller and took the tv back to the main menu of the game system. A breath of relief was released from the lungs of each as they began to nervously laugh at the excitement.

"Must have been a loose connection between the plug and the wall," Jake sighed as he crawled over to the outlet behind his dresser. "That's weird. The plug is in the wall, and everything is connected where it needs to be."

"I wo--wonder how everything turned off and back on by itself," Eric stuttered.

"It was probably just a power surge or something like that," Stephanie reassured.

"Bu—But what about the reflection of that boy in the tv? And it sure got cold in here really fast!"

"Probably just a trick of the light, and the nerves in our bodies playing tricks on us because of our fears" she added.

The kids soon calmed down and tried to relax once more. Stephanie skimmed Jake's comic books. Eric messed with Jake's skateboard, rolling it back and forth across the floor with his feet. Jake laid on the floor and tossed his baseball up toward the ceiling, catching it when it came back down and returning it to the air.

"You guys wanna go to the creek in a bit," Eric asked as if he were bored.

"Yeah," Jake agreed as he continued to toss the ball in the air. "That could be fun. Do you guys swim down there? Or fish? Or do you just hang out?"

"We usually swim there," Stephanie answered without taking her eyes away from the Xena comic she'd been reading.

"Yeah, we've got a tire swing strung up from a branch over the water and a plastic tarp stretched out along the bank to act as a water slide," Eric announced. "It's usually really fun!"

Jake tossed his baseball into the air once more, but when it came time for it to fall back into his hands, it just hung there. It was as if time had stopped. He hadn't really been paying close attention, just going through the motions. But when the ball didn't return to his hands, his attention immediately became focused on it.

"What the..." His eyes locked onto the ball as it seemed to hover in mid-air. Eric and Stephanie turned their attention to Jake when they heard this and followed his eyes up to the ball. As soon as they saw it hanging in the air, their jaws dropped in astonishment.

The skateboard rolled quickly out from under Eric's feet. Stephanie dropped the comic book on the shelf and stood there stiff. Jake raised himself without taking his eyes off what was going on.

Their eyes nearly went wide in shock at the sight of the floating ball. None of them could believe what they were seeing. Everything stood still for the three. The ball just hung there, unmoving, and then began to spin on its axis. First it spun horizontally and then vertically. It was slow at first, but gradually it sped up.

Their eyes grew wider and wider, focusing all their attention on the floating object. Their mouths stood agape with astonishment. It eventually came to a sudden stop, and they watched as it began to float across the room. It went from directly above Jake, all the way across to the doorway and stopped. As the three sat straight up, as stiff as boards, the ball shot across the room and into the closet.

BANG!

All three kids shot to their feet and sprinted out of the bedroom as the sound of a child's laughter could be heard by each, filling the air. Their feet carried them as fast as they could across the floor and down the stairs. As soon as they reached the front door, Jake grabbed hold of the knob and called out just before leaving the house, "Mom, going to the creek with the others be back later!"

He didn't wait for her to respond, but he knew he was to be home in time for dinner. Family dinner was a ritual in the Whitney house. No matter what, they always sat down to dinner as a family and talked about their day.

Jake knew his mom wouldn't have believed him if he'd told her what they just witnessed in his room. He swung the door shut behind him, as they quickly jumped down the steps from his porch and onto the sidewalk that leads up to the house. Jake got about halfway to the street before he realized he needed to get his bike off the porch.

He turned around and sprinted back up the steps to his bike. It was locked to the railing so that no one would take off with it. He wasn't sure if people were as bad about stealing things here as they were in his hometown, but he wasn't taking any chances.

Jake quickly wheeled his bike down the steps and jumped on, while Eric and Stephanie waited for him at the edge of the road. They both looked as if they were about to wet themselves. Their legs quaked as Jake peddled toward them.

"What the heck was that," Eric exclaimed.

"Your guess is as good as mine," Jake replied

None of them could believe what they had seen. First there was a boy behind them in the reflection of the tv, then the baseball just floated in midair. The tv turning off and back on again. And, what about the laughter they had heard as they ran out?

It would seem that the legends about the house were true after all. The house really is haunted. It was creepy while there in that moment, but thinking back about it, it was also a cool thing to experience.

Though Jake hadn't believed in ghosts before, he couldn't deny what they had all just experienced. Eric and Stephanie ran across the street to their houses and grabbed their bikes as well as let their parents know where they were going. Sitting on his bike, leaning on one leg placed on the ground for balance, Jake couldn't help but return his attention to his house.

It wasn't just his house he began staring at, but his bedroom in particular. What the heck was that up there? How in the world did his ball just float in midair? Who was the boy in the reflection and where had that laughter come from? What had his parents gotten him in to?

Thoughts of the house and the legends that follow it filled his mind. Was it all true? Is his house haunted? As he eyes darted across the front of the house, something in his bedroom window caught his eye. He wasn't sure if it was a reflection or the way the way the light cast upon it, but he could swear there was a boy standing in the window looking down at him.

Within just a few short moments, Eric and Stephanie both met back up with Jake, whose attention seemed distracted. They tried to talk to him, but he never acknowledged their return. Finally, Stephanie shook him out of whatever trance he'd been in and he looked at them.

"What's up," Stephanie asked Jake.

"Just thinking," he replied. "For a second I thought I saw someone in my window. There's no way that really just happened right?"

"I don't know," Stephanie responded. "Eric and I both experienced it too. We didn't see the boy in the window but the other stuff seemed pretty real to us."

"There has to be some kind of logical explanation though," Jake rebutted. "I mean, ghosts aren't real!"

"Seemed pretty real to me," Eric said.

"Do you think your parents would let you sleep over tonight," Jake asked Eric.

"Wait what? You don't seriously believe I'm gonna go back in there do you?"

"Oh, come on man," Jake plead. "We can do our own investigation of the place; you know like on that show where they hunt for ghosts."

"Uhhhh," Eric stuttered as he thought about it.

"You gotta do it," Stephanie chimed in. "I would if I thought for one second that my parents would be ok with me staying the night at a boy's house."

"Ok, ok fine," Eric gave in. "But the only way I'm doin it is if we convince Blake and Hudson to come too! Four sets of eyes are a lot better than two. But you guys better not try to scare me or pull any pranks!"

"Alright," Jake agreed. "You got a deal."

"Hey yeah," Stephanie exclaimed. "I've got some walkie talkies you guys can use to keep me up to date. I can use my binoculars to watch from my room. Just make sure you leave your curtains open.

"Alright," agreed. "It's a deal. When we get to the creek, we'll ask Blake and Hudson and then I'll ask my parents."

The trio rode off on their metal steeds like a gang of western outlaws on horseback. As the wind blew

against their faces and the sun shined down upon them,
they all but forgot about the experience they had just had.
There were so few of these summer days left, before they
start back to school, and it was time to enjoy them.

A short while later, they arrived at the creek to find Blake and Hudson already there swinging from the embankment and into the water. Jake, Eric, and Stephanie all parked their bikes next to a large oak tree and got ready to jump in. All the boys had to do was remove their shirts and sneakers. Stephanie on the other hand was wearing her shorts and t-shirt over a one-piece bathing suit, so she had to take them off. She did this and placed them neatly folded in the front basket of her bike.

Eric ran over to the tire and swung out as far as he could before doing a back flip into the water creating a giant splash. Jake on the other hand took a running leap toward the plastic tarp which was spread out along the embankment and slid on his belly down into the water. Stephanie joined them, by just jumping in. She got the idea while in midair, to bring her knees up to her chest and perform a cannonball, which splashed everyone in the vicinity.

Jake didn't have anything like this where he use to live. The closest thing to it, was a water park where you had to pay to get in and even then, you had to wait in long lines just do go down the water slide or jump off the diving board. This was great! No waiting, just a bunch of kids having fun.

After a while, Eric told Blake and Hudson about what had happened in Jake's bedroom and explained about the three of them staying the night and doing some ghost hunting. At first, the boys were a little apprehensive and didn't really believe him, but eventually they got on board. Even if the story Eric had shared with them was false or the three were just trying to prank them, staying the night in a supposedly haunted house could really liven things up.

"That actually sound pretty fun," Hudson exclaimed.

"Yeah," Blake added. "I've never actually experienced a haunting before. I'll have to bring my night vision goggles!"

So, it was a plan. The boys get permission to sleep over at Jake's house and Stephanie would keep a watchful eye from her bedroom and listen in using walkie talkies. They were going to find out what was going on in that house tonight, one way or another. Stephanie only wished she could be there with them, because it sounded like a lot of fun.

"So, what are you guys going to do if you do see a ghost," she asked.

"Well," Jake replied. "I thought I could record it using the video camera on my phone."

"But if it's dark," Hudson interrupted. "You're not going to get much."

"Don't worry," Blake said. "I can use a couple of my dad's infrared lights. They turn any camera into a night vision camera. He uses for night photography."

"Cool," Jake said.

The kids spent the next hour or so horsing around in the creek. They all felt excited to see what the night would bring for them. Everyone was confident their parents would be ok with the sleepover, and Stephanie was even going to try to sneak out as soon as she thought her parents were asleep. It was a great plan. Blake and Hudson were really looking forward to seeing a ghost or experiencing something paranormal.

As the sun rose higher in the sky, everyone decided it was time to get out of the water and head home. It had to be afternoon by this point, and they were all hungry. While at their respective houses, they could then ask about the sleepover and get stuff together. Blake had a spirit board he's been wanting to try out and tonight seemed like the perfect time to do it.

Hudson had always enjoyed telling scary stories around the fire anytime he would go camping. Tonight, seemed like it might just provide excellent material for future campfires, especially if they really do see a ghost. But it wasn't just that that he was looking forward too, he also considered himself a bit of a prankster and wanted to see if he could scare the others.

Eric was a little more hesitant idea. He wasn't at all looking forward to experiencing anything like what they had earlier. But he also didn't want to be the odd one out either. If something was going to happen, he wanted to be a part of it so that he would have stories to tell in the future too. But he made Blake and Hudson agree to not pull any pranks on him, to which they both reluctantly agreed to as they crossed their fingers under water.

When Jake got home after spending most of the morning and early afternoon at the creek, he fixed himself a plate of pizza roles and grabbed a soda from the fridge. It was an hour, or two past lunch time and he was starving. Skipping breakfast plus the activity of riding his bike and swimming on top of an already late lunch had his stomach in knots.

He wasn't looking forward to going up to his room by himself to change and put it off as much as he could. He took each bite very slowly, making sure to dip each roll into a decent amount of ranch dressing on his plate and then shoving it into his mouth to saver it as long as he could. Most of the water from the creek had dried in the wind on his way home, but there was still some that dripped from the seat of his shorts onto the kitchen floor.

About the time he was halfway through his plate, his mom and dad both came into the kitchen. Mr. Whitney went straight for the refrigerator to grab two cold cans of soda. Mrs. Whitney walked over to the pantry so she could grab a bag of potato chips.

"Did you have a good time with your friends," Jake's dad asked as he handed his wife one of the cans.

"Yeah," Jake said taking a swig of his soda pop.

"What'd you guys do today," his mom asked, tearing into the bag of chips.

"Oh, nothin much, just went swimming at the creek."

"You guys be careful down there ok," his dad directed. "I don't want you guys going down there if it rains the night before. I grew up here, and one of my friends almost drowned at that creek because she went swimming after a heavy rain fall."

"How," Jake asked but before his dad could respond, he piped up again. "Wait, you grew up here?!"

"I sure did. But before I get into that let me answer your first question. When it rains a lot, the creek can't move the water downstream quick enough, so the water rises. When that happens, the current begins to move faster and faster. When my friend went in there, the water swept her downstream. A bunch of us were with her, and my girlfriend at the time went after her. But the current was too strong, so they screamed for help. The rest of our friends were off doing something and couldn't hear them. It was up to me to get to them and try to help without going under myself."

"But you're hear now," Jake interrupted. "So, you guys must have gotten out.

"Yeah," his dad responded. "But I nearly drowned in the process. But that's a story for another day."

"So," Jake said. "What about the other thing? You used to live here in town?"

"Yup, I grew up in this very house."

"Wait," Jake said confused. "What?"

"It's true. I grew up here. My parents and I lived here until I graduated high school. Then when I went off to college, mom and dad thought the place was just too big for them, so they sold it. When I found out the middle school needed a new principal, I immediately checked to see if this house was available. Then low and behold, it was. So, your mom and I talked about it, and I applied for the job. We didn't wait to hear back about it, because there were several other schools in the area I could have applied at, or I could have gone back to teaching. We bought the house immediately."

"Did anything creepy ever happen to you here," Jake asked.

"Nothing out of the ordinary. You have to remember; this is a very old house. Before grandma and grandpa sold it, it had been in our family for generations. So, you'll have some creaking floorboards and doors that squeak with the smallest movement. Pipes will knock and the furnace will shoot out strong gusts of air on occasion. But nothing scary ever really happened here."

"Oh, ok" Jake said reassured. "Hey, would it be ok if a few of my friends stayed over tonight?"

"How many are we talkin," his mom asked.

"Just three," Jake replied.

"One of them isn't that cute little red head is it," his mom asked with a slight grin.

"Mom," Jake exclaimed. "No of course not! And she's not cute, she's just a friend!"

"Ok, ok! Just checking," she reassured with a smile on her face.

"I guess that would be ok," his dad agreed. "Just don't be too loud, ok."

"Don't worry, we won't."

With that, Jake finished his pizza rolls and downed the rest of his soda then tossed the can in the garbage and started to run out of the kitchen, but before he could take two steps, his mom tossed a dish towel to him which draped around his face. "First, clean up the water you got all over my floors," she smiled as he pulled the towel down. Once he soaked up all the water leading from the kitchen to the front door, he left the towel on the staircase banister and ran upstairs.

It wasn't until he reached his doorway that he remembered what had scared him, Stephanie, and Eric out of here so fast this morning. He stopped suddenly before crossing the threshold. With one hand on the entryway and the other down at his side he cautiously peaked in.

His door was still wide open from when they had rushed out of there in a hurry this morning. Hesitantly, he stuck his head through the doorway to see inside. He turned his head to the right and then to the left. There wasn't anything out of the ordinary in there. The baseball that had been flung into his closet was still exactly where it had landed, so that was a good sign.

He returned to an upright position and stepped inside. His eyes darted around the room to check for anything he hadn't noticed when he peaked in. But everything was exactly as he had left it. Jake went over to his dresser and pulled out a fresh pair of clothes then got changed after closing his bedroom door.

Shortly after he pulled on his shirt, Jake heard a creek come from inside his closet. It sounded like someone standing on one of the floorboards. When he turned around to see what had made the noise, he was reassured that no one was there. He took a sigh of relief and reassured himself.

"It's an old house," he quoted his dad. "There's gonna be some creaking and strange sounds. Nothing to worry about. There's no such thing as ghosts."

The quiet of his room sent a cold chill up his spine. He heard a squeak come from the floorboard which startled him, but then he realized it had just come from the one he was standing on. As he stood looking around his room once more before opening the door and heading downstairs, all his senses were heightened. A slight breeze flowed in through his opened window which caused the curtains to move ever so slightly.

At any moment, he expected something to happen. Maybe his ball would come rolling out of his closet toward him. Maybe he'd hear another creek or squeak. Maybe he'd catch the reflection of that boy once more in his television screen.

The tv! The moment he thought about that, the image of what he and his friends saw that morning played back in his mind. His eyes locked onto it as he waited for something to happen. He took a deep breath, and his nerves began to dance around, filling his gut with paranoia.

Everything was still. His eyes started to dry from staring at his reflection it the tv screen. His body tensed. It was almost as if he had become a statue. A tingling sensation crawled up his back like a dozen spiders making their way to his head.

DING DONG!

He nearly jumped out of his skin when the doorbell rang so loudly throughout the house. Old houses were like that, the doorbells had to be loud back then. Apparently, no one had ever updated it. He took one final look around his room before he pulled his door open and ran downstairs.

"Jake," his mom called out to him not realizing he was already hopping down the stairs. "Oh, there you are. Your friends are here."

Eric, Hunter, Blake, and Stephanie all stood at the front door. The boys held their over night bags down at their sides and looked in with unease. Stephanie stood behind them, almost hidden. If something was going to jump out at them, she was going to let it get the boys first, she mused in her head as she peaked around Hudson's head.

"Well don't be shy," Mrs. Whitney stepped aside and gestured. "Come on in."

"Hey guys," Jake said stepping from the stairs. "I take it your parents said it was ok?"

The boys nodded their heads up and down as their eyes rose to Jake's bedroom door at the top of the stairs and to the right. When Stephanie realized they were all being ridiculous, she pushed through and stepped inside. A moment passed, and when nothing happened to her, the boys each stepped forth.

They weren't sure what they expected to happen as soon as one of them entered. Would doors slam? Would they hear disembodied laughter or screams? Would they see apparitions walking the halls? How ridiculous they thought.

Mrs. Whitney went to the basement to begin laundry as Jake directed his friends upstairs. He got halfway up when he noticed no one else was coming up behind him and the front door was still open. He looked at the group and sighed deeply.

"You guys comin or what? It's ok, I was just in there and nothing happened."

The boys looked at each other as Stephanie stepped up after Jake. The next in line up the stairs was Eric who directed the other two to shut the door before they come up. Hesitantly, Hudson inched forward as Black turned and shut the door before continuing right behind his friends.

The two were just entering the large house for the first time felt a sense of eeriness as their eyes darted around along their way up the stairs. Everything appeared nice and normal inside. They hadn't really been sure what to expect before they entered, but they didn't think it would be so warm and welcoming.

At the top of the stairs, they each turned; one by one and marched into Jake's bedroom. Stephanie peaked her head into Jake's closet to make sure there was nothing hiding around the corner, ready to jump out at them. Eric bent down and looked under Jake's bed for the same reason. Blake and Hudson dropped their bags next to the doorway and stood turning the heads rapidly, darting their eyes around the room, waiting for some kind of apparition to come barreling through a wall or dropping down through the ceiling.

"Look guys," Jake announced. "There's nothing here! I was just in here by myself, and nothing happened to me."

It was at that time, the baseball on Jake's closet floor rolled to the middle of the room. All five kids looked down at it and the blood in their veins ran cold. It seemed as if the temperature in that room dropped about thirty degrees in less than a minute.

"There's definitely something here," Stephanie said quietly, breaking the silence. Feeling a chill on her arms in the moment, she wrapped her arms around herself and looked at the others. Eric looked as if he forgot to breath. Blake and Hudson's jaws hung open in a ghast. Jake quickly tried to shake off his surprise.

"It's an old house guys," he exclaimed. "It was probably just sitting in a floor pocket and the extra weight from everyone in here shifted one of the floorboards just enough to make it roll back out."

"Oh yeah," Eric spoke up. "What about earlier? How the heck did it float in midair and then fly into the closet?!"

"I don't know, but I don't think it's ghosts!"

"That reminds me" Stephanie said as she handed a walkie talkie to Jake, that she brought with her. "Here. It has brand new batteries, so keep it with you all night. And don't forget, keep the curtains and blinds open so I can see what's going on."

"Sure," Jake replied as he took the device from her and stood it on his dresser.

When they finally got over the shock of the baseball rolling on its own, Hudson and Blake started looking around Jake's room. Hudson showed an interest in all of Jake's different masks, while Blake quickly dug into his comic book collection. Jake, Eric, and Stephanie sat on the floor and played one of Jake's video games. About an hour later, Mrs. Whitney came up the stairs and checked in on everyone.

"How're you kids doin up here?"

Almost in unison they all replied without taking their eyes away from whatever they were doing, "good."

"I was thinking about ordering pizza tonight for dinner. Is that ok with everyone?"

The boys all nodded in agreement.

"Stephanie, will you be joining us for dinner?"

"Sure," she said looking over at Jake's mom. "If that's ok with you."

"That's perfectly fine. Just make sure your parents know, ok."

Stephanie nodded with a smile and Mrs. Whitney went back downstairs. She couldn't help but think how nice Jake's parents were. She had met his dad only briefly, earlier in the day, but he seemed like he was going to be a lot better principal than their last one.

That evening, everyone enjoyed pizza downstairs. The kids all sat on the living room floor biting into the cheesy goodness while watching episodes of Alfred Hitchcock Presents and the Twilight Zone to really get them in the mood for what was to come. While the friends hung out in the living room, Mr. and Mrs. Whitney ate their pizza at the dining room table and shared in adult conversation.

A short time after the friends had all stuffed themselves and it was getting further and further into the evening hours, Mr. Whitney walked Stephanie home. Even though she just lived across the street, it was dark outside, and he didn't want anything to happen to her between their house and hers. This also gave him an excuse to introduce himself to her parents and his new neighbors.

When Stephanie and Mr. Whitney left, the boys all went up to Jake's room. Eric walked over to the dresser and turned the walkie talkie on, then pressed the hands-free button. Jake went over to the window facing the street and pulled the curtains open, after which he raised the mini blinds. Blake went to his bag and pulled out the infrared lights he borrowed and gave one to each of the guys to attach to their phones so they could use the video feature to have evidence of ghostly activity in the house.

Across the street, Stephanie opened her front door and called to her parents. "Mom, Dad! Mr. Whitney from across the street is here!"

A moment or two later as Jake's father stood outside on the front stoop, Stephanie's parents came to the door. Her mom had red hair and freckles and looked just like Stephanie only older and with short hair. Her dad was a larger guy, some would say he was a true working-class man as he was about six feet tall and nearly three hundred pounds, with dirt under his fingernails and tan lines that showed exactly what type of shirt he wore to work, and where his sunglasses sat on his face.

"Hello," they greeted their new neighbor as they opened the door to welcome him in.

"Hi, I'm John Whitney. We just moved in across the street and I'm going to be Stephanie's new principal this year. Stephanie and my son Jake have become friends and she's been spending a lot of time at our house, so I just thought I'd introduce myself."

"Why hello! I'm Mary Parker and this is my husband, Peter. We hope Stephanie hasn't been bothering you too much."

"Oh no," Mr. Whitney said. "She's been a pleasure. I'm just glad Jake met some friends so fast. He was pretty disappointed to leave all his friends back home."

"Well, we're glad she's made him feel welcome," Mr. Parker stated shaking Mr. Whitney's hand. "What brings you to town? Surely you and your family didn't move here just to be a school principal."

"Well not completely," Mr. Whitney said. "I actually grew up in the very house we just moved in to. When I heard the school was looking for a principal I checked to see if my family home was available and here, we are."

Mrs. Parker raised her hands to her mouth in recognition. "Oh my gosh, you're that John Whitney?!" He looked at her a bit confused. "We went to school together! My name back then was Kent."

A smile of recognition spread across Mr. Whitney's face as he put his hands on his hips. "Well, I'll be," he said. "You actually stuck around here huh?"

Mrs. Parker smiled widely in remembrance of all the adventures they and their crew went on as they were kids. "Yeah, I'm a lifer. What are the chances that our kids would hit it off," she stated rhetorically. She immediately leaned in close and whispered, "have you told them about you know what?"

"Not yet," he whispered back. "But I think they're close to finding out."

As soon as Mr. Whitney and her parents started talking, Stephanie went to her room. She grabbed a pair of binoculars from atop her dresser and the other walkie talkie from her bedside table. Opening her miniblinds, she turned the radio on and held the binoculars up to her eyes, aimed directly at Jake standing in front of his bedroom window. "Can you guys hear me over there," she said into the device.

"We can hear ya loud and clear," Eric's voice came back as Jake waved to her.

"Ok great," she exclaimed as quietly as she could. "Just keep me posted ok. I'll leave my radio on."

As Stephanie sat on her bed and turned her tv on to pass the time, Jake shut the bedroom door and turned out the lights while Eric lit a few candles. Blake pulled the spirit board from his bag while Hudson grabbed his night vision goggles.

"This is a spirit board," Blake said quietly with a hint of doom in his voice. "It's used to talk to the dead. If there are ghosts here, this will let them communicate with us."

Hudson placed his goggles over his eyes as Blake laid the board out on the floor and they all sat around it. He directed them how to handle the lens in the middle by putting two fingers from each hand on it but letter the rest of you go limp. The goal was not to move it at all, but rather let the spirits take over. On the board were two curved rows of letter and below them a row of numbers. In the top corners, were the words Yes and No, and at the bottom the words Hello and Goodbye.

The lens they used to allow the spirits to make out words, was a simple wooden hexagon with a clear piece of glass in the center. The hexagon would move around the board and the lens would stop over whatever letter the spirit directed it to. Eventually, the letters would make out a word or sentence for the kids to understand.

"To the spirits of this house," Blake announced as everyone placed their fingers on the board. "Are you there?"

For a moment there was nothing. Silence filled the room. The light of the candles around them flickered as the still air turned into a mild breeze flowing through the room. The curtains which hung against the sides of each widow moved against the wall and suddenly extended outward as the flames of the candle went out.

The boys looked around the room as they felt it grow cold. Jakes parents had gone to bed shortly before they started, and footsteps could be heard across the downstairs floor. Tingles climbed up their backs as the curtains settled back to rest. The lens they held with their fingers that was called the Eye slowly shook to life and began to move.

The boys' attention quickly returned to the lens as the Eye moved. At first, they were in shock as it slid slowly across the board. Each of them swallowed deeply as their eyes locked on the movement.

"Ok," Jake blurted out. "Who's moving it?"

Each of the boys looked at each other. They all shook their heads to say no without moving their mouths. Suspicion pushed to the surface of Jake's face he developed a knowing grin.

"You're moving it aren't you," he said looking directly at Blake.

"Uh," Blake choked.

"What about you," Jake asked accusingly as he turned his eyes to Hudson.

"Noooo," he replied as he held onto the o sound a little to long, not believing his eyes.

"Well, someone's gotta be moving it! Is it you," Jake asked Eric.

Eric's jaw dropped and his mouth fell open, but no words came out. When he realized this, he quickly shook his head no.

The Eye stopped over the word YES.

"What's going on over their guys," Stephanie's voice said over the walkie talkie. Across the street, she held her binoculars up to her eyes and tried looking into Jake's bedroom window. However, it was far too dark inside to see anything but the reflection of streetlights shining against the glass.

"IT MOVED," Eric announced.

"Well, what'd it say," Stephanie questioned.

"It said YES," Jake chimed in skeptically. "But I think someone's moving it."

"What's your name," Blake asked the board.

Once again, the Eye slid across it. Each of the boys looked on in surprise, except for Jake who was a little more cynical. The Eye would move briefly before stopping on a letter and then it would move again. Time and time again this would occur until a name was spelled out. The letters it selected were J-O-S-H-U-A.

"Joshua," Stephanie's voice said over the radio as she had been writing each letter down as the boys said it allowed each time the Eye stopped.

One she spoke the name, the Eye moved once more. It slid quickly to the top left-hand corner and stopped over the word YES. The boys gasped in surprise at such a human sounding name. They weren't sure what they had been expecting, maybe something that sounded a bit more supernatural in origin, but Joshua wasn't it.

"Why are you here," Hudson spoke aloud.

Immediately the Eye began moving again. It slid across the board and stopped briefly on the letters it needed. F-U-N, were the letters the Eye picked out.

"Fun? What's that suppose to mean," Stephanie questioned again.

"Maybe it's trying to say," Eric spoke up. "It... it's having to much fun scaring people who move in here."

"Is that what you mean," Hudson asked.

The board gave no response. The boys waited for something to happen, but the Eye on the board never shifted. Not a single sound was made, nor a single object moved. They weren't sure what to make of it. A moment went by and then two, three, four. Finally, a voice came over the walkie talkie and broke the silence.

"FUUUUUUUUUN!"

The voice which bellowed out from the device was deep and jarring. It sent shivers down each of the boys' arms and a chill up their necks. Simultaneously they all turned their heads to look at the box without taking their fingers off the Eye.

"Stephanie," Jake exclaimed curiously. "How the heck'd you get your voice so deep?"

"That... that wasn't me," she returned.

At that moment a gust of wind blew through the Jake's bedroom windows. Immediately following this, the door to his room flew open and the boys jumped nearly out of their skin. The blankets on both of Jake's bunk beds lifted into the air and flew to the middle of the room, dropping over the boys like a parachute.

Each one of the boys quickly lifted their fingers from the Eye and pulled the bedding off them. About the time they were free, the lights in the room flickered on and off. It was a strobe of light igniting the darkness and made everyone seem to move like watching a movie frame by frame with half the frames cut out. The spirit board rose from the floor and hovered before their eyes.

"Guys," Stephanie's voice exclaimed over the radio. "What's going on over there?!

She watched from her window as rays of light flashed from Jake's bedroom window. It looked like a war was going on but was contained within that space. Everything in her told Stephanie to stay in her room, but curiosity got the better of her.

Rising to her feet, she dropped the binoculars and walkie talkie on her bed. Grabbing her tennis shoes from the closet she pulled them on. She grabbed a flashlight from her bedside table, raised the window and quietly climbed out it; so as not to alert her parents. Her feet carried her across the lawn and over the street, coming to a stop in Jake's front yard.

The front door was probably locked, how was she going to get inside? Fortunately for her, she happened to find a ladder laying on it's side along the foundation of the Whitney's house. Stephanie raised it up to Jake's bedroom window and placed it securely against the house. Her hands and feet worked together, to carry her upward toward her friends.

Everything in her was telling her no. Her fear of heights wanted to keep her flat on the ground. Her fear of ghosts wanted to keep her as far away from all the action as possible. And her fear of the unknown made her wish she were back in bed.

Higher and higher she climbed. Adrenaline pushed her onward and upward. She just had to know what was going on up there. Rung after rung she climbed.

First, she moved her hand, then she moved a foot. It went on like this for what seemed like an eternity. With every rung she climbed the ground moved further and further away. She felt herself grow dizzy as adrenaline and nervousness mixed inside her.

About halfway up, her eyes happened to look down. For the first time she realized just how high up she was. The ground spun beneath her as she pulled herself close to the cold unsteady metal. She could feel her heart thump faster and faster against her chest. The nerves running through her caused her arms and legs to shake as she felt her balance begin to shift.

"Oh no," she thought as she tightened her grip. She felt like she was going to fall. Anxiety rushed through every part of her body. She couldn't move, she wouldn't move. Stephanie held herself as flat against the ladder as physically possible, trying her best to hang on and regain control.

Sweat beaded across her forehead as her palms grew wet and began to slide. She was losing her grip and if that happened, she would surely fall. Was she high enough up that she could possibly die? She wasn't for sure, but one thing she knew was if she fell, she'd would absolutely break one of her bones.

She had to release one of her hands from the ladder and wipe it against her side and then grab back hold and do the same with the other one. She was just to scared. She didn't want to fall! As her hands slid further apart and came to a rest against the sides of the ladder, she could feel her grip begin to loosen.

Stephanie clinched her eyes shut and took a deep breath. She had to hurry up and calm herself down. She needed to dry the palms of her hands and get up this ladder! She let out the breath she had just taken in and slowly pulled her right hand from the ladder and wiped it on her shorts, removing as much sweat as she could then returned it to the rung. She performed the same action with her left hand, but instead of returning it from where it had been, she reached for the next rung up.

That was it! She could do this! Stephanie alternated once again, between hand and foot. Up the ladder she climbed, this time more slowly than she had before. Within a hand's reach from the windowsill, she stopped and again took a breath, her eyes once more glanced down and the ground seemed miles away.

Once more she pulled her body tight against the ladder. But this time, one hand was hanging on to the ledge of the window above her while the other was pressed close against her. Just then, a hand reached through the opened window and grabbed her wrist.

The swirling a sheets and blankets along with the flickering of lights and the astonishment that the spirit board was floating in midair, combined with static coming out of the walkie talking, took all attention from any trace of Stephanie's voice coming through the device. The boys were awestruck and the expressions on their faces showed it.

The board spun around and around as it floated. The lights continued to strobe on and off. A continuous gust of wind bellowed through the open windows. The drawers on Jake's dresser even began to slide open and bang closed. In and out they repeated on a loop as the boys pulled themselves to their feet in panic and disbelief.

The door to the bedroom banged open and closed repeatedly. Jake was certain all the noise had woken his parents up; but as of yet there had been no sign of them at his bedroom entry way, wondering what the heck was going on. This all went on for what seemed like forever, but in reality, had only been about five or ten minutes at most.

Eventually, all the chaos settled down and everything came to a rest once more. The bedroom light remained on, and the door shut, the wind stopped, and the dresser drawers closed. Even the spirit board fell to the ground. It was about that time Jake noticed a hand holding on to the bottom of the windowsill, with fingers gripping tightly on the inside of the frame.

Jake inched toward the window to investigate the strange hand that dug its nails into the wooden ledge. As he got closer, he noticed the top of a ladder resting against the house. Slowly he angled himself to peak out the window and down toward the ground. That's when he noticed a terrified Stephanie hanging on for dear life.

Jake directed the others to come help him. Gazing at him in shocked confusion, they eventually did as he asked. Eric, Blake, and Hudson all gathered around the window and noticed the same thing Jake had. There was their friend, the only girl of the group hanging onto the windowsill with one outstretched hand and hugging the ladder with her other.

The boys grabbed hold of Jake as the upper half of his body went through the opening of the window. He looked down at Stephanie and knew how scared she must have been. His room had after all, been on the second floor of an old house. And with everything that was going on inside, he really couldn't blame her. He outstretched his hand and grabbed hold tight of Stephanie's wrist.

Altogether, the boys pulled Stephanie up the ladder and inside Jake's room. She gratefully thanked them as she made her way onto the solid floor and away from that ladder. She took a deep breath of relief as she looked around and dropped to the floor, her back against the wall.

"What the heck happened over here," she asked as she wiped the sweat from her forehead.

Just as the boys were about to answer, everybody turned their attention to the bedroom door. They could hear footstep creaking up the staircase. Each step squeaked underneath the foot of whoever it was that climbed the stairs.

Once more their hearts began to race as fear froze them in their tracks. There was nowhere for them to go as the sounds got closer and closer. Even Stephanie had a hard time not thinking the worst was on the other side of that door.

In all the excitement, not once had Jake's parents come to his room, so he knew it couldn't be them. Had they been awake, the noise the bedroom produced would have surely drawn their attention; but it hadn't, so Jake knew they were still in their room, sound asleep. The eyes of everyone in that room grew wide with dread as they couldn't help but wonder what was next.

CREEEAAAK... SQUEEEEAAAAK... CREEEEAAAK... SQUEEEAAAK... CREEEAAAAK...

The footsteps had gotten to the top of the stairs and were now making their way toward this very room. Though they were quiet, the sounds of the floorboard creaking, and squeaking seemed to echo throughout the house. Behind them Jake's masks rose from their resting places and slowly drifted toward the group without their knowledge. Jake had several creepy masks among his collection that floated toward the. There were a couple evil clowns, a zombie mask, a werewolf, a devil face and even a creepy jack o' lantern; and all of them were heading their way.

The footsteps in the hallway moved ploddingly toward the room and came to a stop just outside Jake's bedroom door. It was at that time each member of the group stood like statues and held their breaths as the doorknob turned.

Their eyes grew wide as the hinges of the door began to squeak. The door creaked open, ever so slowly. By the time it came to a stop against the inside wall, everyone in the room let out a gasp.

The doorway was empty as the friends stared on and their mouths fell open. They weren't sure what to make of it. There was no one there. The silence was deafening, and their muscles were tense. Standing there agape, the friends waited for next frightening thing to jump out at them, all the while unaware of the masks levitating behind them.

Jake could no longer be a skeptic. Everything he and his friends experienced tonight, made him believe. He now realized that ghosts really do exist and the very house he was now living in, **WAS HAUNTED!**

He had to tell his parents, but would they believe him? He hadn't noticed them acting any differently lately. Could he and his new friends be the only ones experiencing this paranormal activity? Surely a house as haunted as this one, wouldn't only attack the kids. He was certain the ghosts of this house wanted his family out of there, as quickly as possible and without hesitation.

His throat took a deep gulp as he looked on. A million thoughts ran through his mind. None of them could just stand here forever waiting for whatever it was to jump out at them. He had to make a move. He had to got wake his parents and tell them they all needed to leave as fast as possible. But could he force himself out into the hall without knowing what awaited him?

Blake, Hudson, Eric, and Stephanie were frozen stiff with fear. They couldn't believe what was happening. It was at this time they all realized what had happened to Shady Grady. He must have been forced to finish out his contract as principal of the school, and with no where else to go, he was stuck in this haunted house until the end of the school year. It must have drove him insane!

Just as Jake began to move his foot and step forward into the unknown, a voice echoed through the darkness. Once again Jake's body went stiff. It was a female voice and the words it screamed were **"NOOOOOO!"**

The sound of it sent shockwaves through them as they remained as still as they possibly could, their mouths still wide open and their eyes nearly bulging from their heads. A few seconds after the disembodied voice shrieked at them, their eyes fell upon a horrific sight.

A transparent woman with long flowing dark hair and wearing an old-fashioned gown came into view. She hovered in the doorway nearly a foot off the ground. If the apparition had feet, the kids certainly couldn't see them. What passed as skin for a ghost, appeared very pale on her. She had dark circles around her eyes and an expressionless face.

The woman seemed to look past the kids and finally opened her mouth to speak. "Joshua put those away and leave them alone," she directed to the space behind them. It was at that moment the friends turned around. Drifting weightlessly in the air were each of Jake's creepy masks, just inches from their faces.

The kids were shocked by the sight and out of reflex, jumped backward in the direction of the female ghost. The masks then dropped to the floor and the ghost of a young boy appeared before them. Unlike the woman, he had a complete form. He stood in front of them in an old dark outfit that looked as if it came from Victorian England. His hair was even combed into a short dark bowl cut on his head.

A moment later, a voice dame from the doorway behind them. They quickly realized the female ghost was still there and they were surrounded. But the voice which spoke up wasn't a woman. It was deeper than that but comforting. Jake immediately recognized it as his dad's voice.

"I see you've met our housemates," Mr. Whitney said.

Jake and the others turned to once again lock eyes with the lady ghost. Jake's dad and Stephanie's mom were standing on either side of her. Mrs. Whitney was directly behind her husband and Mr. Parker was behind his wife. The group were stunned as their shoulders slumped and began to slouch forward. Stephanie and Jake's parents smiled back at them as the ghost between them developed a warm and welcoming expression on her face.

"Kids," Mr. Whitney said. "I'd like you to meet Jake's great grandmother, Alice Whitney."

A gentle voice came from the apparition's mouth, directed at them. "And the mischievous little boy behind you is my son, Jake's great uncle, Joshua Whitney."

Several moments later, the group of friends were all gathered downstairs with Jake and Stephanie's parents as well as the ghosts of Jake's great grandmother and her son, Jake's great uncle. Mr. Whitney explained that their house had long retained the spirits of the much older Whitney's. When Jake's dad moved away, the family didn't want to sell the house, but it was just too big for Mr. Whitney's parents. The spirits which walked the halls there were family and they couldn't leave with the couple, so they were stuck.

Mr. Whitney had grown up with the knowledge that his family home had ghosts within. Often, he would play with Joshua and even introduced the spirits to his friends. One of those friends was Stephanie's mom. At first it was a little creepy for them, but they quickly got use to the spirits and included Joshua in everything they'd do that was inside the house.

When Mr. Whitney found out that Joshua had been scaring away all the home's residents ever since the family left, he just knew he had to find a way to bring it back into the family and keep it this time. Mr. Whitney knew the previous owner was the principal at the local middle school and began the process of buying the house long before Mr. Grady left. He introduced himself to the man about midway through the school year and told him he'd be happy to buy the house and even take over for him as principal as long as he waited until the end of the school year to move.

Mr. Grady got all his affairs in order and put in a good word for Mr. Whitney with the school superintendent. In the weeks leading up to the last day of school, Grady began moving his stuff out of the house in the middle of the night. As soon as school let out on the last day before summer break, the Whitney's closed on the house and got a call from the school superintendent telling him he got the job if he still wanted it.

All five friends were aghast to learn the truth. It took them a bit of time, but eventually they got use to the idea of ghosts ever present in the house. Eric, Blake, Hudson and yes even Stephanie spent much of their time over the years there and often stayed the night. Joshua was always among the first to tell the group creepy ghost stories.

Imagine that... Being told a ghost story by an actual ghost!

In the room where the group of friends learned that ghosts exist, the spirit board laid. It rested on the floor, a simple object that could easily be mistaken for a children's toy. The quiet of the room surrounded it. Papers which had blown around only minutes earlier and masks which had floated behind the kids settled around the room.

The sound of boards creaking eventually broke the quiet of the night. The simple game in the middle of the room, slowly began to quake. A shadow slithered across the floor, coming to a rest on the board. The light over head flickered dramatically as a slight breeze blew through Jake's bedroom windows.

The curtains which had hung lifelessly in front of said windows, gradually began to rise, pushing toward the center of the room. The breeze wasn't coming from any single direction though, as every curtain, in front of all the windows seemed to move in the direction of the board. Every last one shot straight out around it, almost as if the board itself had reached out with invisible hands and pulled the curtains toward itself.

Jake's masks soon changed in expression. Where most of the masks once resembled faces with wicked grins or terrifying screaming features, and some held and angry growling appearance, they each now wore an expression of horror. The masks had distorted to resemble a declaration of fear. The masks were afraid of what was to come.

The posters around Jake's bedroom, plastered across his walls, each made a similar metamorphosis. Horrified expressions of terror wiped across anything with a face. Baseball cards and comic book characters shared in this as eyes of characters seemed to move in the direction of the board.

Once more the room went still. Everything seemed to freeze in place. The curtains all stuck straight out, the masks on the floor stiff with dread. The light bulb which hung from the ceiling got brighter and brighter.

A slow-moving cloud of icy cold air moved into the room from the windows and doorway. It crept across the floor and drifted toward the center of the room. Coming to a brief stop over the board, it rose, filling the room in an impenetrable frosty fog.

Beneath the cloud were slithering vines, creeping in from the outside. They skulked through the windows undercover of the icy mist. Resembling the fingers of a wicked witch the vines scratched across the floor.

The light overhead reached its brightest and then everything went black. For a few seconds the room was as dark as a crypt and just as lifeless too. Not a sound could be heard, nor could an object be seen; that is, if there were anyone looking in to see it. Looking into the room from the hallway, a passerby might think there were a pitch-black curtain hung in the doorway to remove the room from sight.

Of course, there was no one around to witness this strange occurrence. Everyone who resides in the house had gone downstairs, both living and dead alike. What could possibly have caused this eerie sight. Had the house been haunted by more ghosts than originally let on? Could the board itself have been brought to life?

When the light came back on, the room had been empty. All of Jake's stuff was certainly still exactly where he left it. However, the icy cold fog had left and with it, the vines which had slithered their way in. The curtains once more hung lifelessly in front of the windows and not the slightest breeze could be felt entering the room.

Everything seemed to have returned to normal. The characters on posters, trading cards and comics had returned their facial expressions to exactly as they had originally been depicted. The masks too, had returned to their original form. But there, in the center of the room, in the middle of the floor, no longer rested the spirit board. Mysteriously the board was gone.

A few weeks later, the group of friends had been visiting the neighborhood rummage sale. There were tables lining the street, packed full of all kinds of things for sale. There were tables which clearly belonged to certain households while others seemed more communal.

The community tables were filled with things that had gone unclaimed. Such things as objects from the lost and found or city property that had been stored in a community building for years on end. There were retired street signs up for sale, and damaged traffic cones, tools which had long been replaced, coats, shoes, bags, and other things which had been taking up space for years.

As the friends walked along the street and browsed the tables for goodies they might want, Blake noticed at the end of the road there sat a table. The table was all but empty. He moved closer toward it, with his friends following behind. The closer they got, the more Blake noticed, the table wasn't empty at all.

There in the center of it with nothing else around, laid an object which creeped him out. As he stood directly in front of it, his eyes fell upon it. He wasn't sure at first, but upon closer inspection, as his friends gathered round, they all soon realized it was the spirit board they had used that eerily fateful night.

ABOUT THE AUTHOR

S.M. Cornthwaite has a degree in Psychology with a strong interest in true crime and the paranormal. He lives in Central Illinois with his wife and children, where he spends much of his time reading, writing, and studying. Cornthwaite has long wanted to tell stories and has many of them to share. Much of these, draw upon elements and experiences from his own life and the legends of his hometown.

The author began the Hollow Screams book series, shortly after publishing his first true crime book and while working on the first installment of an adult horror book series. His goal is to captivate his readers beginning during their early years and keep their interest as they grow into adulthood. All his stories may not appeal to everyone, but it's his desire to present something for each age group, so that his readers may enjoy his stories, throughout their lives.

All the stories in both the author's adult horror anthology series as well as the Hollow Screams series are interconnected. You'll find references of all different sizes between the two series. This of course was done purposefully by the author, to keep those who've read the Hollow Screams series reading his books, long into adulthood. But it was also done so that parents who read his adult horror series, can also enjoy Hollow Screams with their kids.

www.ingramcontent.com/pod-product-compliance
Lightning Source LLC
Chambersburg PA
CBHW052042150726
48002CB00002B/719